Toni Hunt, born in Solihull in the Midlands, grew up in Sutton Coldfield and moved to Hampshire in 1995 with her ex-husband and two children. Her main occupation is in education working as a high-level teaching assistant at a local school and her ambition was to write a book about her journey with her autistic son. *Autism… A Mother's Story* is her first book and covers almost 28 years and she hopes it will gain insight into the complexity of autism. Toni remarried in 2012 and lives happily by the sea on the South Coast and continues to offer care and support to her son and enjoys spending time with her two grandchildren.

To Stephanie
for often taking a back seat.
To Peter
without whom this book would not have been possible.

Toni Hunt

AUTISM...
A MOTHER'S STORY

AUSTIN MACAULEY PUBLISHERS™

LONDON • CAMBRIDGE • NEW YORK • SHARJAH

A CIP catalogue record for this title is available from the British Library.

ISBN 9781398443648 (Paperback)
ISBN 9781398443655 (ePub e-book)

www.austinmacauley.com

First Published 2023
Austin Macauley Publishers Ltd®
1 Canada Square
Canary Wharf
London
E14 5AA

First of all, I would like to say a very heartfelt thank you to Austin Macauley Publishers for offering me this opportunity to see my story in print. There have been many individuals and health professionals throughout Peter's life that have been of great help to Peter, myself and us as a family, so would like to thank you. Hopefully, you will know who you are and how you've helped. A big thank you to Michael Davies, Independent Educational and Neuropsychologist HCPC for allowing me to use part of his report in my book as I feel it played a valuable part in the telling of my story as well as being a pivotal part in how things worked out for Peter. My appreciation goes out to The Right To Work (CIC), who has given Peter the chance to try supported volunteer opportunities which has improved his self-esteem and well-being. Thank you to Andy, my husband for all your support over the years and for agreeing to read my story even though you hate reading! Thanks to two friends that were the first to read my manuscript and urged me to find a publisher. In memory of my late father, who provided financial support when I needed it. A huge debt of gratitude goes to Stephanie, my daughter who has been a source of support over the years… I know it's not been easy. Finally, thank you to Peter for making this story possible, without you I would not be the person I am today.

Table of Contents

Note from the Author

My story is one that many parents of autistic children can relate to. It is not designed to give you in-depth knowledge of the condition but mainly to share my experiences with you.

It has been a journey of huge ups and downs, but I am hoping that by recounting my experience you may gain a greater understanding of the daily struggles of autistic children, adults, and their carers.

My journey spans from 1997 to the present day. My son is now 28 years old but for me, the struggle is not over, and know it will continue until the day I die. You never stop worrying about your children, regardless of their circumstances but being a parent to an autistic child requires a lot of determination and hard work, something I never knew I was capable of until I had Peter.

The early years before diagnosis, was a period of knowing something was wrong, but being extremely ignorant of what it might be. We had no one in our family with any sort of disability and we were extremely clue-less as to what a disability was. Post diagnosis was a period when I felt that I was more a carer than a parent and this has continued into adulthood.

As I have now grown into my role, I am a strong advocate for his care, his finances, and his medical requirements.

During this section of my story, you may gain valuable information that may help you on your journey.

Childhood Years:
The Beginning

"I think your son is Autistic," said the Speech and Language Therapist.

I remember thinking but he's not in a wheelchair. As you can gather from this first thought response is that I had no idea whatsoever what Autism was. It was 1996 and we had, at last, made our way to the top of the waiting list for speech and language intervention. This was only an assessment and I had been waiting eight months to get to this point.

As a family we had moved down to the south coast in 1995 when Peter was just over two years old, his sister was seven and I was thirty-five. By early 1996, I approached the Health Visitor attached to my doctor's surgery as I was concerned by his lack of speech. His speech had progressed quite well until 15 months old when he would say mum, dad, drink, banana, and baked beans. From 15 months he lost all speech and was using the word 'gegah' for a drink.

I took away his dummy and enrolled him in nursery convinced that his speech would take off. This unfortunately was not the case.

This was all new to me but the start of a journey that was now to become my life. The health visitor was able to sign post me to various professionals, including a hearing assessment (which came back normal), but the waiting list for speech and language was excessively long, so was referred to a Child Health and Developmental service which was a new child health provision and had no waiting list. It quickly became apparent that Peter also had other developmental delays and was referred to a paediatric doctor.

The words spoken by the speech and language therapist felt as if they were meant for someone else. I was ignorant of the word 'Autism', how I wished my husband had attended the appointment with me, not that I think he would have been any more prepared than I was at the time. I can't remember how I found out more about this condition as we didn't have a computer, but I soon became somewhat of an expert in this new word and jumped on a roller coaster towards the unknown.

Sleepless Nights

In addition to Peter's verbal delay was his inability to sleep. What I am about to recount here now makes me smile, but sleep deprivation had a profound effect on our lives.

At bedtime, Peter loved a story, and we would spend a considerable amount of time on this routine each night. He would often fall asleep but during the early hours, he would spend most of the night awake and alert often making squeaky noises.

Peter loved his story tapes (it was 1996 after all) during the night. He enjoyed most Disney stories, Thomas Tank, Roald Dahl, and many others. His favourite at one time was Beauty and the Beast, but the tape was only ten minutes on each side. So, every ten minutes I would have to get out of bed to change over the tape, which would often last hours into the night. My husband seemed oblivious to the constant movement in the bed but would often comment he had also had little sleep. I remember feeling very frustrated at this. Why had he not got up to help just once?

Anyway, I decided to tape this story onto a cassette that lasted 45 minutes on each side. Success! Two days later, he no longer wanted to listen to the tape and moved onto another Disney story. As with most autistic children and even adults, there is an obsession with people, films, and objects and Peter was no exception. He has progressed through life with many fixations, some bordering on the sinister and macabre.

Peter didn't sleep during the night until he was seven years old, he always stayed in bed, but we relied on these much-needed stories to get him (and us) through the night.

Barney, the Coat and No Coat

Most children whether autistic or not have obsessions with items of clothing. My daughter had one with her wellies and would insist on going to bed in hers for a week.

Peter was no different and his was a Barney t-shirt. Just as he was obsessed with his story tapes, he also loved Barney the friendly dinosaur which he loved to watch on a videotape. I'm not quite sure where this t-shirt came from but how I wished at the time, we could have purchased more. Despite trying we couldn't source another t-shirt the same (black with a purple Barney on the front).

This t-shirt was worn every day for what seemed like months on end; he would go to bed in it, and I would have to take it off whilst he was asleep, wash it and have it ready for when he awoke during the night. He was quickly growing out of it but try as I might he would not take it off and I was unable to find another one. I even thought that if I bought a plain black shirt whether there was anyone who would produce a Barney onto it. Today, I would imagine this may not be too difficult, but at the time didn't seem possible, especially as we were extremely short of money.

The day came when the t-shirt went out of favour, and he preferred to wear a navy-blue coat instead. This coat would have to go on once he was dressed in the morning and remain on regardless of the weather (indoors and out) until he got ready for bed in the evening. As you can imagine, the coat became very dirty throughout the day, so again this had to be washed and dried ready for the next day.

Of course, the day came when he no longer wanted to wear this coat or any coat whatsoever. However hard we tried; we couldn't get him to wear a coat again for many years. He didn't seem to notice if he was hot or cold and no matter how we tried to reason with him he would not wear any sort of outdoor garment apart from a sweatshirt that belonged to me which he took a shine to because of its tactile feel.

Today, he will wear black providing it has some sort of transfer on it, whether this be a character from a film, television programme, or his favourite pop idol. Even in hot weather, he prefers to wear black and refuses to wear shorts.

Fiddle Objects
and Obsessive Traits

Those who are familiar with autism; have children or know someone who cares for a child with this condition, will recognise their reliance on fiddle objects.

The reason for writing this book is mainly to share my experience with you, not to impart any real knowledge as each child is different. I know that some children with autism are non-verbal, are incontinent, suffer extreme developmental delays, are sensitive to noise, are unable to feel pain, and refuse any offers of comfort.

For Peter, his reliance on fiddle objects quite simply got him through the day. He would often hold an object up to his eyes, tap it on his nose, drop it, dance around it, and pick it up again. One of his objects was a grey piece of plastic that had fallen off an item of furniture or something similar. We are not sure where it came from, but it was with him all the time. He took it to school, bed, and on holiday.

He once lost it at school, and everyone was out on the school playground looking for it. We were on holiday and whilst throwing it and dancing around it on the balcony of the apartment, he accidentally threw it onto the beach just below. There was a quick run around to the rock pools on the beach and we luckily found it. He still has that piece of plastic today and occasionally uses it to fiddle with.

He seems to get some sort of comfort from the tactile feel of an object, the shape of how it feels in his hand, or how it looks when he holds it up to his eyes. For Peter, it helps him make sense of the world he is in or a welcome distraction from the reality of life.

When Peter was younger, he would love the sound of the vacuum cleaner, washing machine, lawnmower, and hose in the garden. I would often watch Peter with his toy lawnmower walking alongside his father whilst he was mowing the lawn. We had an extremely large garden, so this task would take over an hour. Sometimes, he could not bear for this to end and would become extremely distressed. We sometimes fell into the trap of continuing a chore even though it was completed to avoid this catastrophic meltdown.

Pre-Diagnosis

Following the speech and language assessment, Peter began his therapy sessions. By this time, he had been in nursery for over a year and was observed to be very withdrawn. He would often just sit on his own in a corner and would not interact with staff or other children. The staff there were concerned and encouraged me to push for an autistic assessment.

We managed to get an appointment with a Paediatric Doctor, and I voiced my concerns, telling her about his behaviour at nursery and urged for her to refer him for an autistic assessment. She was a lovely doctor but persuaded me to wait another six months as the waiting list was long. I remember asking why we couldn't just go on the list and if things improved, we could always come off it. Writing this, I feel so cross with myself that I wasn't more forceful.

Behaviour

At home, he didn't want to leave the house and it took us many hours to get him in a car, which would nearly always end in a violent outburst, hair pulling, and biting. We had to resort to giving him two-minute warnings. This invariably was more like two hours at first, but by reiterating these time scales, he would be more relaxed knowing that at some point he would be leaving the house. It took lots of encouragement and coaxing to get his feet measured for new shoes. This could sometimes take an hour before he would eventually go inside the shop. He was very particular about the items of clothing he would wear. He didn't like stripes or patterns or anything black (apart from his Barney t-shirt), blue or white. He would not allow for his hair to be cut and it took many hours of persuasion for him to allow me to cut it. He would not let anyone else do it and as a result, he ended up with a 'basin' cut as he couldn't bear for clippers to be used. I now know that children with autism are very touch sensitive but most of the information available at the time focused mainly on lack of eye contact, slow speech, and lack of social interaction. Peter's obvious distress made perfect sense to me once I stumbled on this new piece of information.

If someone turned up at the house unannounced, he would not be able to cope, and this would end in a massive meltdown. This was particularly difficult for my daughter as she liked to have friends to visit, but during this period it just wasn't possible. Once the two-minute warnings were in place, visitors to the house were slightly easier.

As time went on, his violent outbursts became more commonplace and was a real concern for the professionals we were in touch with. Once, while sitting in the waiting room for Peter's speech and language session, he viciously attacked me. He punched and pulled my hair with such force that handfuls of my hair came out in his hand. He was deeply distressed, and I would suspect that this was his way of telling me that he didn't want to engage in these sessions as they made no sense to him. This scenario prompted an immediate social services referral to help assist us as a family.

Not All Doom and Gloom

Despite, our lives being turned upside down, we tried to have a normal family life. Even though it was hard for us to get Peter to leave the house, we always persevered and wouldn't allow him to become isolated at home. We invited the family to stay, we went on holiday, and we visited friends. We always gave him time warnings, so he would know what was expected of him. He was a very loving child, but we noticed his lack of eye contact. Every evening at about six o'clock Peter would run around the house at racetrack speed, mainly on his tiptoes and using his fiddle object, dropping it on the floor, dancing around it and picking it up and hitting his nose with it. This routine would usually last for a couple of hours and little could be done to stop it. It became difficult to watch the television as he was constantly jumping in front of it. However, when Peter was ill (which wasn't very often), he would not have the energy to do it, and this was a welcome respite for us.

We noticed during this time, that Peter had an amazing memory. He would often alert us in his way that he had been somewhere before, and we realised that he had but when he was much younger. He would be able to tell us about railway barrier crossings, the correct way to a place of interest, and all the characters in his favourite movies. He would also only walk into town a certain way observing all the burglar alarms on the buildings. If we attempted the walk a different way, he would have a huge meltdown.

At this time, we noticed that although Peter's language was delayed, he would often repeat the last thing we had said and would do this constantly. And so, I found out a new word 'echolalia' (meaningless repetition of another person's spoken words), which occurs in many cases of autism spectrum disorders.

Diet

During this period of pre-diagnosis, we noticed the food that Peter had previously loved was now off the menu. He would continue to eat cereal but would be eaten at every meal if he had the choice. His lunchtime sandwiches had to be jam or marmite. He would not eat fruit or vegetables but would have a plate of meat for Sunday lunch. He loved McDonalds and would happily devour a 'happy meal' providing it was chicken nuggets and chips. Chips, though, were not accepted at home.

During the summer we introduced Peter to ice-creams and lollies which he found extremely difficult to eat. It ended up all around his face and down his clothes. Even today at twenty-seven, he still struggles to eat these items of food and will often avoid having them.

Obsessions

Peter's fascination for Disney characters continued which initially was mainly due to the little toys you could get in a McDonald's 'happy meal'. These toys were ideal as fiddle objects due to their small size. Once an obsession was fully blown, he just needed to find a toy for him to take out with him. If we couldn't find a toy, he would ask for me to draw a character onto cardboard, so he could use that instead. As the fixations progressed, he would begin to recite the dialogue from a film or programme insisting that we fill in the gaps of the other characters. His memory was amazing, and we still recount a scene from a Simpsons episode that he loves.

Lara Croft

One Christmas my daughter had a PlayStation and Peter adored watching people play their games on this console. It soon became apparent that even though Peter was unable to cope with the remote control due to his lack of dexterity, he would be able to direct us on the best way to progress to the next level or how to solve a puzzle. Lara Croft on Tomb Raider was ideal for this, and he would happily sit, watch, and advise.

We realised that Peter could become quite addicted to these games, so gave him half an hour twice daily during the week and a little longer at weekends. He still observes this time scale today.

Christmas and Birthdays

Family celebrations are normally happy and relaxed, but for Peter, it was a day that didn't follow the normal routine and it could end up extremely stressful.

From an early age, Peter had to be told to open his presents. He was not a child to just delve into his gifts. He had to be shown how to accept a present, rip off the paper and enjoy the moment. He was incapable of this, and his gifts had to be spread out over several days as he just couldn't cope with them all at once. His face rarely showed any emotion except when he received a gift that was his current obsession. He did however love putting up the Christmas tree and fiddling with the different decorations and listening to Christmas music. We always managed a visit to Father Christmas which became less stressful as the years passed and Peter still believed until he was 15 years old.

Today, he is a very thoughtful present buyer and really thinks about the gift he is giving.

Returning to Work

As most of my time was taken up with Peter during the day and childcare would have been a problem, I decided to work in a wine shop a few evenings a week. My husband and I were not well off, so I thought the extra money would come in handy. Unfortunately, though this only lasted about six weeks as my husband couldn't cope with putting Peter to bed at night and I also felt guilty that I was enjoying some time away from the home as I was beginning to feel quite isolated. Luckily, my neighbour was a pharmacist and she managed to find me a Saturday job in the local chemist. This worked much better for the family and Stephanie would come and meet me for lunch. I think this was easier for my husband as he would just let Peter watch films most of the day, which wasn't ideal, and I began to feel fretful that I was not there to make sure Peter had a good weekend.

Educational Psychologist

Peter's follow-up appointment with the Paediatric Doctor arrived and I was still being told that an autistic assessment was not possible but was told that he was being referred to an Educational Psychologist who would make recommendations regarding Peter's schooling as he would be five the following March.

This charming gentleman came to our house and observed Peter's behaviour whilst carrying out several tests. The Educational Psychologist witnessed some violent actions during this visit as Peter was continuing to display severe distress when an unknown person visited the house even though we had warned him.

The visit lasted a couple of hours and once the gentleman left, I felt exhausted but didn't think any more of the visit until he called the following week.

The Phone Call

"I am going to start a Statement of Educational Needs (now known as Educational Health Care Plan) for your son," explained the Educational Psychologist.

I was confused because the initial thought that came to my head was that they could not 'section' my son. I was deeply distraught, and the gentleman explained what this statement consisted of. I was now given a new term for me to investigate and by the time the process started I knew what to expect and offer my contributions to this procedure to get the required outcome.

As far as the Educational Psychologist was concerned, Peter had a Speech and Language Disorder, and a short period within an educational establishment that was able to address this was all Peter needed. He didn't believe Peter was autistic and he would probably be able to go into mainstream school after two years.

Grandparents

It became obvious during this time that whilst one set of grandparents were keen to understand Peter's difficulties the other set would simply not accept there was anything wrong. Whether this was because they didn't see disability as something that they wanted in our family or just plain ignorance, it became an exceedingly difficult time for myself and my husband. We wanted friends and family to be supportive and not to put unnecessary barriers in our disruptive life. Whenever we tried to talk about his Statement of Special Educational Needs, his Paediatric Doctor, or his Speech and Language Therapist, they would simply just not want to listen.

Final Statement

The final statement, once completed, recommended that Peter attend a mainstream school with a specialised speech and language unit. This school was about 10–12 miles from our family home, and it was explained that he would be eligible for a taxi and escort each day to transport him to school. He was due to start in September when Peter was four and a half years old. He still seemed extremely young to be starting school but as a family, we were relieved that at last there was light at the end of the tunnel. After all, the educational psychologists had advised that Peter would make progress and would be able to go to a mainstream school soon.

Starting School

Peter started school in September 1997 and we were full of hope that we could now begin a new phase in our family life that looked incredibly hopeful. We had attended an open afternoon at this unit and met some amazing staff, but Peter did not cope with any of the Transition days, so we decided to see what happened in September. The lady in charge of the unit had worked within an autistic residential home and was knowledgeable in the field of autism. Of course, we weren't particularly interested in this as Peter only had a Speech and Language Disorder. She signposted us to an organisation called AFASIC (Association for All Speech Impaired Children).

School Escorts

Trying to get Peter into the taxi at first was very traumatic for him and we were still giving him the 'two minutes' time warning. At first, Peter became aggressive with the escorts, but this soon settled down. If the authority changed taxi companies and escorts, this would also be a problem for Peter as he relied on consistency and familiar adults.

Over the years, we had some lovely escorts who must have been quite dedicated, as Peter was not easy at first. One escort knitted a little dog coat for our dog at the time.

First Month

Peter's first week at school was very traumatic. His behaviour at home initially improved dramatically during the first few weeks, but at school, he was exhibiting extreme behaviour and was soiling and wetting himself constantly and would become distressed when staff tried to clean him up. Peter, however, would not leave the house for school without some reminder of home. This would be a whisk, a pipe off the vacuum cleaner or an ornament, and of course, his grey plastic fiddle toy.

On the advice of the school, we tried to introduce a visual timetable, like the one used at school to provide structure and therefore to alleviate any anxiety about what was coming next. This was working well there, so we had some symbols at home to prompt him for going out (to avoid the two-minute countdown), bath time, bedtime, etc. Unfortunately, Peter became quite angry that these symbols had made their way into the family home, and he tore them down. This was the start of Peter compartmentalising parts of his life – if he was used to something being at school, for instance, he didn't want any part of it at home. He also didn't want any part of family life (parents evening for example), to infiltrate into the school environment, apart from his fiddle toys.

We were introduced to the idea of Social Stories, which for those of you who don't know is a very simply written story that improves the social skills of people with ASD. This may be to prepare a child for an important transition, such as moving school, a new addition to the family, toilet training and to address the anxieties that may be present. It is read several times a day, for a couple of weeks and by this time it will hopefully imbed the changes. This was received far better for Peter in the home (even though it was shared in school also) and this prompted me to attend a course so that I could write my own stories to further help him.

One day, we were called into the school to be told that they thought Peter was autistic. This was a huge bombshell as our hopes of normal family life were being snatched away from us. The teacher who had worked in an autistic setting told us he was exhibiting extreme autistic behaviour and she was recommending that he be seen by the school doctor to start the process of an autistic assessment. My husband and I were dumbfounded. That word 'Autism' had reared its head once again and we were feeling just a little bit confused.

School Doctor

Peter was still displaying autistic behaviour and associated behaviour problems within the unit. He was given one-on-one support and was told that the appointment with the School Doctor was just a formality as the staff within the unit were utterly convinced that Peter was on the autistic spectrum. Unfortunately, this was not as clear-cut as we had all predicted because on the day of the appointment, they sent another doctor in place of the one they had been conversing with and she said his problem was just poor parenting and behavioural problems!

At this point, I had no idea who to believe. We were given so many mixed messages and the professionals that you put your trust in had the ability to turn your life upside down. I now know that this was only the start.

Paediatric Doctor

I entered a new phase during this time, I was proactive in doing as much for my son as was physically possible and so insisted that I have a follow-up appointment with the Paediatric Doctor who we had seen in the past. I was determined that I would insist on an autistic assessment, and I was not going to take no as an answer. I didn't care how long the waiting list was, I was determined to be on it.

Peter and I arrived for this appointment, and I believe she could see by my body language that I was unwavering in my desire for this assessment. She told me that I was not to worry and that she had already put Peter forward but warned I would probably be waiting at least nine months. It was then I realised that they can only put so many forwards for this assessment each year and Peter had reached the top of the list.

This made me feel relieved and angry at the same time because I had to go through all the emotional turmoil to get to this point. Did they not realise that as a family we were at a breaking point?

Pre-Assessment

The process of an assessment at this time (1998), was not a straightforward one as we first had to attend a pre-assessment to see if he was eligible for a formal one. As you can imagine, I was very apprehensive as I was convinced that another barrier would be put in our way and thought that they may refuse our request for a full assessment.

Peter attended this appointment with his latest fiddle toy – a dinosaur. As soon as the professional saw Peter fiddling with this in front of his eyes and tapping it on his nose, she told us that Peter was clearly autistic, and he was put forward for a full assessment but was warned again that there was a long waiting list.

Marriage Breakdown

I do not think that the breakdown of my marriage was due to Peter's disability, but it certainly didn't help. Peter's father was often out of work and amounts of money disappeared from our bank accounts to fund an addiction that my husband had developed. Even though we attended marriage guidance, I could not cope with the lack of money and support from my husband. It was hard to be a mother to a child with a disability and a wife to a husband who I felt had lost all interest in his family. It was a difficult decision to make but my husband was more than happy to leave. My self-esteem was incredibly low, and I felt worthless most of the time but managed to navigate a pathway through to ensure my family was happy regardless of our family situation.

Even though Peter adored his father, he would not allow him to visit unannounced. If he did, Peter would just go to his room and hide under his duvet. Any future visits had to be planned so that I could give Peter sufficient warning to help him cope.

Autistic Assessment

Six weeks following the pre-assessment, Peter's appointment turned up for the full assessment. This was nothing like the nine months that had been predicted and as a family, we were so relieved that again we could look forward to the future. In hindsight, there was no difference: there was no magic wand that was waved, where everything was alright, no extra help was offered to us as a family it was just the diagnosis that Peter was definitely autistic.

The day began with myself and my husband talking to a professional about Peter's early childhood and any other family members with a similar condition whilst Peter was observed in the outside area with other children. He was incredibly anxious which is always beneficial during these judgements as the professionals get to see the full picture. It is not however ideal for the child concerned as they can remain in a highly anxious state for far longer than necessary. This was a day that did not follow the normal rules and no matter how hard we prepared Peter for the day was immaterial as we had no idea ourselves.

Following this period of outdoor play, Peter was observed through a one-way window with the specialist involved. My husband and I were treated to lunch and had no further contact with anyone until the end of the assessment. I am not sure how these assessments progress today, but Peter's lasted all day and many tests had to be carried out. Today, I believe there is a blood test that can detect autism.

The final diagnosis was that Peter had mid to high-functioning autism, moderate learning difficulty, and a speech and language disorder.

The day ended with mixed emotions. At last, we had a diagnosis, but we had no idea what would happen now we had it. I remember feeling that at least I was not a bad parent as previously indicated by the school doctor but also feeling like I was sinking into a black hole with no way out.

Post Diagnosis

Peter continued attending the speech and language provision at his school as there was trained staff there that could help him grow and develop. It seemed pointless to move him, but the local authority tried to re-locate him to a special school locally in the area. On reflection, this may have been the better option for him but at his current school there was a highly trained teacher who had so much knowledge and he had made a friend who he adored, and this was a friendship that lasted the duration of his time there.

Disability Living Allowance

I was advised following Peter's diagnosis that I apply for Disability Living Allowance (DLA), which is also known as Personal Independence Payment (PIP). I was told that this payment could help with funding respite care and help with the day-to-day care of a child with a disability. Things such as extra laundry cost as Peter wet and soiled his bed most nights, larger nappies, and having the extra money to enjoy time together as a family. I was shown how to fill the form in and gain the necessary reports from the professionals involved. Peter was awarded a higher rate of personal care as he was awake during the night. At about the age of seven, when Peter managed to sleep through the night, we resubmitted the form and he gained the middle rate of personal care.

Carer's Allowance

As well as DLA, I was advised to claim Carer's Allowance. I was unable to work because of Peter's disability except for a Saturday job that I had started to do before my husband left. This was no longer possible as my husband wasn't always reliable when it came to looking after his children. I recollect feeling uneasy about this as it was my job to look after my son and didn't need to be paid for doing it. However, due to no payments coming in from my husband it was a necessity, at least for the short term.

Family Fund

During this time, I was also encouraged to apply to Family Fund. This is an organisation providing grants for families raising disabled or seriously ill children and is still active today. They helped with the cost of a washing machine, tumble dryer, and a family holiday for several years. We had to apply each year and most of the time we were successful. Without this charity, we would not have been able to enjoy a family holiday together.

Disabled Parking Badge

We had to apply for a parking badge because Peter was beginning to develop an aversion to the concrete in some car parks. He preferred bases that were made of tarmac. It was a bit of a struggle to obtain one on the grounds he was not physically disabled and today this is now starting to move towards allowing those with mental disabilities to have access to this badge as well. We had this badge for 12 months, and we couldn't renew it for the reason already explained. During this time, Peter's dislike of car park surfaces diminished.

School Life

Peter continued attending the speech and language unit and settled into his surroundings. He still had his special friend, and he did make a few others. During his time at this school, he enjoyed the interaction with his school escorts. There were times when he would become violent, especially if there was a change in the adult companion.

It became apparent that Peter liked things compartmentalised. For instance, if there was an assembly at school that Peter was involved in, he was unable to cope with me being there. So much that he would spend the assembly curled up in a ball on the floor. I then started to attend without his knowledge to avoid this catastrophic meltdown. School sports day was the same and, in the end, I had to stop attending as he became traumatised. For his Annual Review of Special Educational Needs, I would need to attend the school without him being there or ensure that if I was in the school building, he would not have the chance to see me. If I did attend at the end of the school day, it seemed obvious that I would take him home instead of his escort. Unfortunately, he could not cope with that either. This continued well until he started college and then he seemed better equipped at seeing me outside of his home environment.

At school, he was observed to have little or no interest in the school curriculum but was able to absorb information that was of interest to him. We were shocked when Peter began telling the time accurately for o'clock, half past, quarter to and quarter past especially as his teacher said he was uncooperative during his lessons.

Phonics was of no interest to Peter, and he relied heavily on his sight vocabulary to pick out familiar words, so his reading ability remains very sketchy which is frustrating for him.

Stephanie

His sister Stephanie was good with her brother and was an enormous support to me and her father when she stayed with him at weekends. However, she became upset when she observed Peter being violent towards me. At times, he would hit me and pull my hair, and this became difficult for Stephanie to witness. It was also difficult for her to have friends visit the house which further distressed her. At this time, child services were heavily involved with us as a family and arranged for a Clinical Psychologist to see her for six weeks to help with her feelings and ways of coping. This helped her, and life plodded on for us as a family of three.

A New Job

Now Peter was at school, I decided to volunteer at our local school (which Stephanie attended), to offer reading support to pupils. I did this several afternoons a week to widen my horizons and to be part of the school community and I found it rewarding. One afternoon, the Head Teacher asked me if I wanted to support the children myself in class instead of reading. I readily agreed, but little did I know that it was a form of an interview. He congratulated me on my interaction with the children and offered me a job as a Teaching Assistant the following September. I couldn't believe it; this was not where I could see myself working as most of my working life was in customer service. This was ideal though, as I could earn extra money (and not rely on Carers Allowance) for some little luxuries and have time off with the children in the holidays. I felt this was a 'win-win' situation.

Holidays

Our first holiday was a camping holiday and the first for us as a family of three. We ventured over to the Isle of Wight, and we had a glorious week. The only problem was that Peter would not consider venturing into the communal washrooms, so his washes would be carried out in the tent. We were lucky enough to be on a campsite with a bathroom and once we had booked in our slot, Peter would happily go in there for a more thorough wash. This camping holiday and others that followed were an ideal time for Peter to join in with the daily chores. He helped with the washing up, shopping for provisions, and keeping our tent tidy.

The camping holidays were a regular feature for us but after a while, we started holidaying with another family that was well known to us. We went on camping holidays and also stayed in holiday cottages. The first couple of days were always difficult for Peter as it didn't follow his normal routine and there were more of us. By the time the holiday was almost over he was more relaxed, and he enjoyed joining in with the activities. Holidaying with others helped Stephanie as she had others to interact with rather than fitting in around Peter.

It was decided one day that we go on a bike ride on a designated bike path. Peter was unable to ride a two-wheeler, so plans were made for us to hire a large tricycle for him. It took us 45 minutes before he would even sit on the bike and once on it, we had to ensure that he steered in a straight line. It was so funny, every time anyone cycled the other way, we asked him to 'stop', because he had no sense of direction and he ended up crashing into other people or bushes. The path was 45 minutes in each direction, so once our ride was over, Peter was much more confident. People often say that autistic people or children are unable to master a two-wheeler bike, and this has been the case for Peter. We did try a tandem once, but even that proved difficult for him. Today, if we go to Center Parcs for instance, he will ride an adult three-wheeler bike, which enables him to join in with everyone else.

On another holiday, we thought we'd give pony trekking a go. Again, Peter did not want to do this at first, but the staff were helpful and offered to walk Peter's little pony in case he decided to give it a go. Whilst walking alongside, he became quite fond of the horse I was riding and decided that was the one he wanted to ride. Yes, you've guessed it, I had to go on the small pony (which was exceedingly small), and Peter trotted along happily on mine.

I have such fond memories of these times and Peter will often recount these adventures too.

Wilson

Stephanie wanted us to have a dog, and this was something that had been going on for many years. As I was now working, we began researching different breeds and we decided on a small cross between a Shih Tzu and Lhasa Apso which turned out to be a good decision. He was a little bundle of joy and Stephanie decided to call him Wilson (the rugby ball from the film Castaway).

When Peter was out walking, it was normally difficult to keep him safe on the pavement. He would sometimes jump off the pavement into the road and I was worried about how I would manage Peter and a dog whilst out walking. From the start, I allowed Peter to hold the lead and to my amazement, Peter was so involved in keeping Wilson safe that he no longer became a danger to himself. He still wanted to follow his familiar route, but walking became an enjoyment for both of us. Wilson also seemed to make Peter less anxious which made life at home a little easier.

Respite Care

It became obvious to child services, that we needed some time away from Peter to have some mother and daughter time. This was a period when we explored various avenues of respite care. We visited a care home where Peter could stay overnight with other children with disabilities. Peter became extremely traumatised by this suggestion and wouldn't leave the car to go inside. In the end, we were signposted towards Family Link which was organised by child services. This involved Peter spending time individually with a person on the family link database. Peter could attend (usually at their house) for a couple of hours. Again though, Peter could not cope with this time away from me and the lady concerned said she no longer wanted to have him.

As time progressed, we were put in touch with a company that had support workers that could offer respite care. This involved them spending time with Peter at home or out in the community for anything from one to three hours and sometimes longer, depending on the support package that was offered by social services. At first, Peter would spend most of the time in his bedroom under the duvet. This progressed from hiding under the duvet and talking to the support worker whilst still in his room, to playing together on the PlayStation and finally going out. At first, it was beneficial to maintain the same support worker to alleviate Peter's anxiousness and as time progressed, he would allow new adults to take him out. We had some lovely support workers that were dedicated to caring for children and young adults with a range of disabilities and Peter began to enjoy his time with them. When Peter got older, he continued to qualify for this service, and he is still in touch with some of his support workers today.

Theme Parks and Places of Interest

As mentioned before, we did try and do normal family things, but sometimes it became quite stressful. I became aware that if I showed evidence of his Disability Living Allowance, we would get a discount for myself as a Carer and had priority access to rides at theme parks. This was especially useful during a family holiday in Florida in 2011. Later, when Peter had a yellow disability card, I was able to get in as his carer. He loved the cinema and without this concession, we could not have afforded to go.

Friendships

Peter's friendship with a little girl lasted throughout his time in the language unit and they were inseparable. Unfortunately, he became over-reliant on her friendship and wanted it to be exclusive to him. He started to exhibit aggressive behaviour if he saw her talking or being friends with someone else.

Peter didn't understand the rules of friendships and very soon his behaviour forced his little friend away. He left this school having lost a very dear friend.

Secondary School

When thinking about a secondary placement for Peter it seemed obvious that he attended a special school near home. The school I chose, appeared to tick all the right boxes with regards to their knowledge of autism and I thought that attending an establishment near home would allow Peter to have friends he could see outside of school.

His transition days were catastrophic. It became apparent that the school had no experience of autism, and these two days were spent with Peter hiding under a chair in the reception with no staff to observe him or coax him to come out. Because there were no adults, Peter wet and soiled himself as he couldn't ask anyone for the toilet.

Once he started school in September, he was given one-on-one support but was still exhibiting extreme meltdowns. Over time, he made a friend (a girl) who seemed to be drawn to Peter in a motherly way. Peter loved this and he became much happier. However, once the girl showed friendship to anyone else besides Peter, he would become extremely violent and on one occasion had her up by the clothes pegs by her throat. This was something we had never experienced before but was the start of a pattern of obsessive friendships.

Once again, Peter's behaviour deteriorated, and it became clear that this school was not ideal for his condition. Most of the staff were not geared up for dealing with an autistic child, they had no behaviour strategies, besides the ones I gave them. With this in mind, I requested a change to his Statement of Educational Needs. You would have thought that this would be easy, but this began a long battle with the local authority that lasted almost two years.

Relationships

It is worth mentioning that during this time, I tried to have time for myself and managed to date again. I had one boyfriend who was recently single and known to us as a family, so it seemed a natural progression for us to start dating. His two girls and my daughter became firm friends, and we had some lovely family holidays together. It was a mutual decision to end this relationship as my boyfriend couldn't understand the bond that I had with Peter, and he began to get jealous of our relationship. Many boyfriends couldn't cope with his autism in general and some gave me ultimatums that either I push for Peter to attend a residential school, or they leave. I had one acquaintance that called him a 'nutter'. No one throughout this time moved in with me and I began to feel a little worthless. I used to love going to listen to live music in pubs and I met many lovely friends both male and female and we used to go far and wide to see our favourite bands. I began to be a free spirit while I was out and not having the restraints of being a mother to an autistic child. It gave me time to breathe even for a few short hours, once or twice a week.

Preparing for Tribunal

The school and the local authorities were not easy to deal with. They were reluctant to amend his statement to allow Peter to attend a school better equipped to deal with his autism. The school appeared to orchestrate reports from professionals in their favour and I felt extremely isolated. When I asked the school, what experience they had dealing with autism they said that having Peter was the basis of their knowledge!

To organise a change in Peter's statement, I had to inform the local authority of my intention. Several meetings with the school and the head educational officer within the council ensued to no avail. Once this hurdle had been crossed, I had to request that his case go to Tribunal. This was a time-consuming and expensive process, and I had no idea how to go about it.

It was a chance meeting at a parent support group where I met the father of a son with autism, who had a similar experience to the one I was dealing with. He put me in touch with an Independent Educational Psychologist who would be able to help with my case.

Educational Psychologist's Report

This experienced professional (**Mike Davies, Independent Educational and Neuropsychologist, HCPC Registered) ***, visited Peter in the school setting and carried out many tests. Some of these focused mainly on expression, reception, and recall of narrative. It was noticed that although he began to say words and sentences, he would not or could not complete them. After a while, he protested that he couldn't complete a task and would often run one sentence into another. The outcome of this was that he scored low in verbal comprehension, perceptual reasoning, and working memory.

Throughout the assessment, he complained that he couldn't complete basic tasks and had great difficulty in his reasoning and was unable to retain answers. Because of this, the educational psychologist started selecting assessments that took a limited time that didn't rely on spoken responses which was an area of difficulty for Peter.

The gentleman tried to conduct a word reading test and found that Peter was unable to read simple words like 'into' or 'so'. Now, some assessors may take this refusal as behaviour related, but it became apparent to the educational psychologist, and he quoted, "Peter has genuine difficulty associated with years of frustration at being taught to sound out words which he clearly can't do, and he has never gained an appreciable amount of sight vocabulary." However, his SAT results from his primary school told a different story which led the gentleman to believe that Peter had lost a skill that he had previously been able to do. A listening comprehension task was attempted because of the low language needed to complete the test. However, Peter was still very resistant, and it took much time for him to respond.

The observations were that "Peter has significant word-finding difficulties, difficulty constructing sentences, inefficient word retrieval and a general reluctance in all language tasks". And that, "Peter has an extremely severe language disorder which is disabling for him and has stopped his educational progress because of its density".

There was one segment of this assessment where Peter was struggling with many words, but he produced a response with the word 'disguise' which many other children who this gentleman had assessed had not been able to produce. This one word gave a level of success equivalent to a 16-year-old. Peter of course was nowhere near this level, but he astounded the assessor by producing this knowledge of vocabulary, despite his exceptional difficulties, which the gentleman reported "Is testament to the conundrum that he faces each day".

It was also conveyed during this day that "The school has removed his speech and language therapy input that was central to the original decision to place Peter in a primary speech and language therapy unit in the first place".

In conclusion, the Educational Psychologist recommended two schools that could assist Peter and advised "That this happens sooner rather than later before his oppositional behaviour becomes even more entrenched". He further reported that "His speech and language is almost impenetrable."

This report didn't come cheap, but was worth it and I used all my savings for this to be conducted. I was fortunate, however, that my father who had taken a keen interest in Peter's predicament (and followed any news or documentaries on autism) gave me the money as a way of replenishing my funds.

*michaelndavies@talk21.com

Documentation and Outcome

Now I had the report, I had to number and document the paperwork in readiness for Tribunal. If at this stage I was unable to convince the panel, I would have to prepare myself for a court case. I had a huge amount of paperwork and I had to number each piece of paper, copy it several times, and send it off to the tribunal dignitaries. I was lucky that I was working in a school, so the Head Mistress permitted me to copy everything I needed. Once the paperwork was sent off, I would receive correspondence from the school and the school would receive my evidence.

I was astounded when I received the paperwork from the school: it consisted only of their school prospectus which massed to about 25 pages whilst my evidence exceeded 200 pages. With my evidence, the local authority backed down and Peter was able to get his statement amended.

Teenage Years
Fresh Start

Peter started his new school which was a mainstream secondary school with an autistic unit attached. Once again, Peter had to be escorted by taxi each day and he soon settled down into school life. The staff at this school were amazing and Peter began making new friends and made progress with his learning.

Peter still struggled to see me in his school environment, so visits for annual reviews etc still had to be made without Peter's knowledge. At home, Peter's aggressive behaviour diminished, and he continued to enjoy time with his support workers on days out. Stephanie and I started to enjoy time out together and I began making new friends to socialise with. It was easier to go out socially because Stephanie was old enough to babysit and neighbours who knew Peter were also happy to do this service for us.

Andy

During early 2008, I was fortunate to meet Andy, who is now my husband. I was initially drawn to him because he had a grown-up daughter who was disabled and thought that at least he would be more emphatic than others that I had gone out with. I had a lot of male and female friends and I only envisaged Andy as being a friend, but soon realised that he was sympathetic to my situation and went out of his way to include Peter on days out. We very soon began dating and I was happy that I had met someone willing to take us on as a package and I, at last, began to feel happy and relaxed in this new relationship. Andy and I married in 2012.

Obsessive Friendship

Peter began to make so much progress in his autistic unit that for a couple of afternoons a week he was allowed to integrate within the mainstream school. At first, this started well, he enjoyed the woodworking lessons and the wider curriculum. He soon gained a new friend with a boy in his year group and Peter began to insist on more time within the mainstream setting. Once again, Peter could not cope that this new friend also had other acquaintances and began to monopolise his attention. He also, wanted to dress like his new friend and insisted on wanting new clothes (even though they were not the colours or designs that Peter would normally go for).

Just before the school summer holidays, the friendship began to dwindle, and other children began to stop Peter from having any contact with him. So, throughout the summer holidays, Peter was obsessed with seeing this boy again and even our family holiday was spoilt because of this preoccupation.

Also, during this summer break, we went to the cinema to see the new Batman film 'The Dark Knight'. I personally found this film quite disturbing even though it was a 12a and I soon realised that it had influenced Peter as well. He began talking as if he were the Joker by reciting phrases from the film. As previously mentioned, this was something he would often do, but all his thoughts were totally on this character, and we began to be quite concerned.

Exclusion

It was the start of the new academic year, and I was quite relieved that Peter was going back to school. Normally, I enjoyed having the children at home over the six weeks but Peter's preoccupation with his friend made the summer quite difficult. I thought the structure of school life would help sort him out. However, on this first day of the school term, I received a telephone call from Peter's social worker. He had taken a knife to school (not a sharp one) and started to threaten a young girl who was a friend of the boy that Peter was obsessed with. He must have been planning this before the new term started and I was astounded by this behaviour and deeply embarrassed. Why had I not noticed? Unfortunately, the police were called, and Peter was escorted home and was not allowed back at school. Even though Peter had been excluded from attending school (which I agreed with), plans were put in place for home tutoring. A member of the school team visited our house three times a week and plans were put in place for Peter to attend a college twice a week especially for children who were not in school or education. The social worker was brilliant and was on call daily to assist with the new predicament we were in. Peter was also put into touch with the CAMS team who prescribed him an antidepressant but unfortunately, this had an adverse effect on him, and he began self-harming. During this time, Peter was still very obsessed with his estranged friend and would often leave the house after his tutor had left for the day (I was at work). He was trying to find his way back to the school so he could see this boy. He became very troubled and very soon it was decided that one tutor working on their own was a potential risk, so a member of the Respite Team was brought in to assist with the home tutoring.

Child and Mental Health (CAMS)

Peter continued to be deeply depressed, angry, and obsessed. He would often try hitting himself over the head with a saucepan. This was exacerbated by the fact that we had sold our home and had not secured alternative accommodation as many had fallen through. Our house had been on the market for over ten months and once a buyer had been secured, I was reluctant to change my mind. Luckily, for us Andy let us live at his house and this was the case for two months. During this time, the tutors still visited, and Peter continued at college for two days a week. Initially, Peter was happy with his new environment and today he still talks about how he enjoyed living there. It soon became apparent, however, that the anti-depressants were not working and a further appointment with the mental health team was requested. The outcome of this appointment was that Peter have access to a mental health nurse who visited once a week at home to offer guidance on friendships, as this was an area of difficulty for Peter. As part of these sessions, it was highlighted that Peter said he didn't like being autistic, so a plan was put into place. This involved him researching various famous people, such as Elton John, Tom Cruise, and Ozzy Osbourne. It materialised that these famous figures had disabilities. Elton John for instance was epileptic and Tom Cruise had some learning difficulties. This made all the difference to Peter, and he began to see himself differently. His medication was discontinued, and a new drug was offered. This drug was called Risperidone, which was mainly prescribed for Schizophrenics, but in a lower dose was effective in dealing with obsessions. The first couple of weeks, Peter was a different person, he was a pleasure to be with and he started interacting more with us as a family. Even though this high was short-lived, we did notice a marked improvement in his state of mind, and his obsession with the boy dissipated.

Community Dentist

Peter had not been to the dentist for a long time as it was a major traumatic episode for him. This was something that couldn't continue, and I was eager to have his teeth checked because if there was a problem, he probably wouldn't experience any pain. We were put in touch with the Community Dentist at our local health centre. I wasn't sure how this was going to pan out, but I gave Peter lots of warnings about what to expect. In the beginning, Peter would not sit in the dentist's chair but on an upright one and he found it hard to open his mouth so the dentist could have a look. Over time, Peter began to sit in the reclining chair and have his teeth checked properly. He was shown how to use floss sticks and he now visits the hygienist every three months. He has even allowed for an impression on his teeth for a mouth guard to wear at night due to excessive grinding of his teeth. It is the kindness and patience of the staff that has enabled Peter to regularly attend his appointments.

Leaving School

Peter continued his home tutoring, and he completed some exams in the home environment. These were mainly entry-level qualifications, and he was disallowed from some subjects due to his autism.

There was some discussion around Post 16 provision, and we were encouraged to visit a school in Winchester, which was about 50 minutes away by car. This was within a special school environment with a separate annexe for post 16's. This involved a residential provision Monday through to Friday and his statement would be maintained by the local authority.

All this was put in place, but then I was informed by some chief official within Hampshire that his statement would not be maintained after all. I was incensed with rage; how could they do that to us? It took many weeks during the school summer holidays to get this decision overturned and, in the end, Peter was able to start when the new term started in September.

Post 16 Provision

Peter was very hesitant when starting this new school and it was agreed that he attend daily at first with the opportunity for him to start residentially when he felt he was ready.

This school was amazing, it was full of dedicated, knowledgeable staff that was familiar with autism and associated disorders. After six weeks, it was decided that he stayed Monday to Friday. He had his own bedroom and shared a bathroom with one other person. There was a rota for cooking meals, cleaning up, and being responsible for keeping his room tidy. As a group, they enjoyed evenings out, social activities within the unit, or just time to relax. Peter enjoyed his time there, and there was a noticeable improvement at home too.

It was quite strange being without Peter during the week, but while he was there, I started to relax and began enjoying activities outside the home. In the past, I had felt guilty going to the gym or going out socially and I was grateful for some 'me' time without these feelings.

The staff at the school encouraged me to claim Employment and Support Allowance (ESA) for Peter. I thought this a bit strange at first, but they pointed out that Peter was unable to work and that was why he was at the unit. They assisted with the application, and he was successful in gaining this benefit in addition to his Disability Living Allowance. After all, they pointed out that Peter was almost an adult, and I couldn't be expected to pay for everything. This released a financial burden on me while giving Peter some of his income, even though he was unable to budget for himself. As Peter was 16, I needed to be approved to be Peter's appointed person for this benefit and his DLA.

During Peter's second year at school, a new boy started, and Peter very much wanted him to be his friend. The boy seemed extremely popular with other students and Peter began to resent this a little. However, there were no repercussions of his obsessions and Peter soon began to accept the rules of friendship.

Peter was due to be at his Post 16 Provision until he was 19, but after the second year, they felt that Peter would not benefit from another year. This came as a blow to Peter as he didn't want to leave his new friend. I'm also ashamed to say that I was very apprehensive. I wasn't sure how things would be with him living back home especially, as he would have nothing to do with his time.

As before, I began taking advice on full-time education opportunities for Peter and other ways that could fill his week without him getting bored or fed up. He was soon enrolled at a college on a course with other young adults with similar needs. This course was to prepare him for working life, self-help skills, money, budgeting, etc. He even joined the drama group and was involved in their performances. I was also advised by the social worker that Peter was put onto the housing register as there was the possibility of a supported living environment that he may be eligible for.

Peter as a baby (about 4 months old)

Peter (9 months old)

Sisterly Love (age 18 months)

Brother and sister together (aged 2-3 years)

Little Poser (aged 2)

Happy Times! (aged about 3 years)

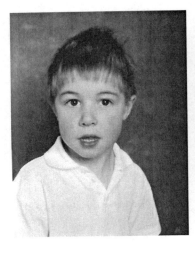

First school photograph (aged 4 and a half)

School Picture (aged 6 years)

School Picture (age 13)

College Photo (age 16)

Prom Picture (age 17)

Florida Wedding

Mom and son out together

Enjoying time after 'lockdown' (age 28)

Early Twenties Supported Living

Following Peter's two years away from home, it became difficult for him to settle back into family life. He missed his residential establishment and his friend. During the holidays I facilitated visits to see his friend, but Peter began to get angry that he was not with him at school.

It took more than a year to finalise his transfer to supported living and Peter could not have been happier. He had a studio-type flat with a kitchen and bathroom and there was a community area to share with other residents as well as a garden for them to enjoy barbecue's etc. There was an area for the residents to do their washing and there was someone there 24 hours a day. The flats were in pristine condition being fully decorated, new carpets and the appropriate white goods fitted. Peter was excited shopping for his new flat and we were grateful for the money from the ESA. We were told the provision was for young adults with disabilities similar to Peter's, so we were confident that Peter would be happy. The only issue was that it was about 20 minutes away by car from the family home with an irregular bus service.

This was our first experience of care workers offering meal support daily living care and a plan was put in place for the support of preparing meals, access to the local community, and the cleaning of his flat. They assisted with Housing Benefit and direct debits, but I decided that I would still be in control of his money.

To achieve some sort of independence for Peter, we decided that Peter could have his own bank account and then a joint account for both of us that his benefits were paid into and the payment of his direct debits. Every week, Peter would receive money into his account for shopping and socialising. Peter felt happy to have this added responsibility and he loved the added freedom of his debit card, which was easier than dealing with money as Peter became frustrated and embarrassed that he was unable to work out how much change he would receive.

Peter would occasionally come home at weekends, and he continued with his visits to his father. We also found a new youth club that Peter could attend, and he enrolled for another course at college. Things were looking positive.

Free Bus Pass

A concession that Peter was eligible for was a free bus pass and this allows him to travel with or without a companion. Initially, he travelled with his support workers until he became confident with the bus route, and we have travelled together enjoying a day out shopping or going to the cinema. Peter is now confident travelling this way and is deeply knowledgeable on the different routes and the various buses he needs to catch.

He has a disability railcard that enables him to travel by train at a reduced cost.

Girlfriends

While Peter was at college, he met a young girl and they decided to go out. This 'going out' was just meeting at college, but Peter was lucky that she also lived close to his support living accommodation. He was invited to have a few meals around her house and there was much texting going on. Unfortunately, though, this young girl then decided that she didn't want Peter around her at college. Peter could not understand this, but the texting continued, and she asked him to buy her a ring. Peter told her it was too soon to talk about any sort of engagement, and she didn't take this too well. It came to a head when she started asking him to take pictures of his private parts and send them to her. Peter knew this was not the right thing to do and he went about it in a very mature manner by telling his Learning Support Assistant at college. The matter was dealt with, and Peter realised that he didn't want to go out with her anymore, so the relationship and friendship ended. This was the first time that Peter had dealt with a relationship issue in such a mature and calm way.

Peter continued going to college and he seemed extremely happy there making lots of new friends. Students and teachers loved his sense of humour, and he became a lover of discos and parties. This social interaction went against some of the attributes of someone with autism and it was lovely to see him grow into an independent and sociable young man. We went to Florida for my brother's wedding, and he was seen strutting his stuff around the dance floor showing off his Michael Jackson moves.

In 2014 he was invited to a birthday party of a young girl he had met at college. Quite a few of Peter's friends went from college and he had a lovely time. Peter didn't see her as a girlfriend so, it came as quite a shock when she asked him out the following week. It started with him going to visit her at her care home and I remember the day I took him there. He collected something for him to eat whilst there and he had found out the buses that would get him back home. He rang me that night and was so happy, telling me all about her. She was in a wheelchair and had quite a few problems communicating but this didn't bother Peter and he soon began to see her every Saturday, where they would watch films in her room and smooching as he would call it. Some relatives found it strange that Peter wanted to be with someone so heavily disabled. I pointed out to them, that Peter liked his own space most of the time, so the relationship suited Peter well. After all, he would never cope with someone knocking on his door every five minutes. Of course, I could sometimes understand where they were coming from as the relationship with his girlfriend was very confined. There would be no walking along the shoreline together or the freedom of popping on a bus to see a film and this saddens me at times. However, after meeting her, I found her to be a fun-loving young girl (a bit older than Peter) and she had the ability to put a smile on your face. As their relationship grew, there were more opportunities for them to go on dates together and

Peter loved it when she was able to go to a disco with him. They are still together today, and I would like to think that sometime in the future they may be able to live together (with support).

Special Talent

It has been stated that some people with autism have special talents, whether that be art or the ability to play or compose complicated music. Unfortunately, Peter does not have that ability, but he has one that uses his interest in films and music.

If you ask Peter when a movie came out, he would be able to tell you the year and the director of that film and tell you how old it is, and he will do the same with music. He will also be able to tell you when your next big birthday will be, how old something is, and how long you have had it. We also realised he could mentally calculate a complex subtraction question but could not tell you what two plus two would be.

Peter is proficient in using the internet, Facebook, Instagram and will play complex PlayStation games. However, mundane tasks, such as cooking and washing up remain an area of difficulty for Peter.

Moving On

After a few years of residing within the supported living accommodation, he told me he no longer felt safe living there. Instead of people with similar disabilities and ages to Peter, the flats were opened to elderly adults and those with quite a few drug problems. He reported that one man kept banging on the wall at night and was often found sleeping in the lift. He said that he wanted somewhere nearer home. The staff advised me that Peter was becoming quite anxious but did say that in their opinion he could live independently with support. What an achievement for Peter, I couldn't quite believe it! Our social worker told us the quickest and easiest way was for Peter to privately rent near our family home, apply for housing benefit, but continue to be listed on the housing register and await a social rented flat. I couldn't quite figure out in my head how this would work but I started searching for a property. The only problem was that the council wouldn't keep him on the register for a one bedroomed flat, but only for supported living. It took many months and an appeal for them to finally back down and change Peter's eligibility to a one bedroomed flat.

Trying to find a property on the housing register was near on impossible, every time I put in a bid, Peter would be 57th in the queue, but we were very lucky to find a privately rented opportunity less than half a mile from home. It was lovely and he had a separate bedroom and a large kitchen/lounge area with double doors opening out to the rear. The rent was the same as his allowance for housing benefit, so it suited us perfectly. The only problem was that as Peter was on benefits, we needed a Guarantor, and I was not eligible as I wasn't earning enough. Luckily, my son-in-law was able to step in and do this and the deal was finalised.

We had to coincide the move to allow for support workers to be assigned to assist him at his new flat and for Peter to have access to a telecare machine that he could use in an emergency.

Even though the flat was perfect, it became evident that there were quite a few teething problems. Due to Peter's lack of dexterity, he found that he was unable to unlock and lock his front door due to the deadlock being quite stiff, so this had to be changed. His bedroom window was a sash window and Peter didn't have the strength to lift it, so we had to fix handles to make this easier for him. The hot water and heating system had no instructions, so I had to download them. For about three weeks, Peter was calling every night with some sort of problem, and I was beginning to feel that we had rushed into this decision and that living independently was not going to work.

However, Peter was extremely happy in his new environment and the care for his meal support was working well also. He was near several supermarkets, and he began to do his own food shopping. Peter was proud of his flat and he loved buying little ornaments and having pictures put up. However, he was not able to do a good clean and we employed a cleaner once a week.

As Peter was now officially an adult, he had to make payments to the county council as a contribution to his care. This involved a person coming to his flat and going over all the relevant benefits that he was entitled to and his outgoings. They allowed for extra expenditure due to his disability i.e., washing (Peter did this at the launderette), chiropody, special clothing, and a cleaner. When this was worked out, Peter would then be charged an amount that he paid monthly.

General Anxiety Disorder

Whether it was because Peter was living alone or the fact that Peter's father suddenly died quite a tragic death, that Peter began to be quite anxious. He would often go back and check he had locked up and switched everything off in his flat. He would become quite fretful when out that everything would be alright when he got back. He began to get angry that his dad had not been a particularly good one. I always made sure that I told Peter his dad was not perfect, but he did the best he knew how. He began telling me I was his 'hero' though, which was nice to hear.

His anxiety increased, so we sought the advice of the doctor who re-referred Peter to the learning disability doctor and access to the Psychiatry service. They requested blood tests and found that the Prolactin level in Peter's blood was off the scale (Hyperprolactinaemia) and they decided to discontinue his Risperidone and put him on Pregabalin which is an anti-anxiety drug, and he was diagnosed with a General Anxiety Disorder. I felt so sorry for him, he was doing so well, but I was worried that perhaps he was alone too much in his new flat. He didn't have access to anybody throughout the day apart from Support workers. He continued though with his youth clubs, and he began to be a supported volunteer in a café and at a country park nearby, potting plants, litter picking, and feeding the animals. This is an organisation *(The Right to Work CIC)* that supports those with learning disabilities prepare for work by offering exciting day service opportunities. He was adamant that he did not want to return to Supported Living or return home to live.

It was about this time the Employment Support Allowance sent a Capability for Work Assessment form for us to fill in. I thought this would be a simple process, but Peter then had to attend an interview. The questions they asked him seemed so irrelevant regardless of his disability or not, but the outcome was that Peter could be moved to the support group with the intention of him finding work, which dropped his payments each month. This meant that he had to attend the job centre regularly in an attempt to find supported employment. This increased his anxiety even further and it became apparent to the job coach that Peter would not be able to work at this time, so his visits to the job centre were rescheduled for every six months. As a result of this, I wrote to the ESA explaining the difficulties Peter was having and whether they could re-access his situation in light of this new finding. They refused and said he would have to wait until his next capability interview! Peter will be the first to admit that he wanted to work and earn his own money, but that someone would need to support him to do this. He did manage to do a little job at HMV for a short time, but this was stopped because he needed too much support.

As part of this General Anxiety Disorder, he started to become angry with the staff at the school he had attended with his friend. One day, I had a call from the police to say that Peter had emailed the staff of his previous Post 16 Provision and made all sorts of threats, so much that they had to put the school on lockdown for fear of him arriving at the school. The threats were quotes from the 'IT' film and they were quite harrowing to hear about. I was stunned that Peter could do such a thing. The police were involved and insisted that Peter send a letter of apology, but no charges would be brought against him, but that this incident would remain on file. The policeman concerned was an Autism Ambassador and he was able to relate to Peter at his level.

For me, there was a significant amount of anxiety because although Peter's flat was extended past the original six months, I was worried about where he would live if his tenancy came to an end.

Special Olympics

Peter was keen to keep his body fit, and we explored many avenues that would suit his needs. He once joined a football club for special needs which was run by a football coach from our local team. He loved going every Wednesday evening, but after a while, this was discontinued.

We were then lucky to find a club that was known as Special Olympics. This is a club that does Olympic-style sports for young people and adults with disabilities. There are many throughout the country and I understand it started in America and it allows its participants to compete all around the country and sometimes abroad. Peter goes training every Monday and he participates in running and long jump. He can earn medals and he greatly enjoys the interaction with others in the club. At first, he was reluctant for me to attend any events, but as time has gone on, he will allow me to see him on the local event days.

Once a year, they have an awards evening and bowling, and he is so proud when he earns a trophy or plaque as a reward for his achievements.

Beechworth Road

Peter's anxiety continued to rise and again was made much worse because his landlord decided to sell his flat. This meant that Peter was on the move again. I had to look for another private rented flat as there was still no joy securing property on the housing register. We were lucky to find another flat around the corner, but unfortunately, private rental charges were rising quite substantially, so his new accommodation was an extra £75.00 a month and his housing benefit didn't quite cover it. Fortunately, the financial team was due to re-access his funds (as he was now approaching 25 years old), and they could allow for the extra money that this new property was going to cost him. Also, whilst looking it was highlighted that a lot of landlords were not accepting those on benefits, so we were lucky to have found somewhere close to the family home.

Before finalising the deal, I used the previous experience of his other flat and made sure that Peter was able to lock and unlock his front door, open his windows, and have all the instructions for the heating system. This flat was a managed property, so the money that had to be paid out for security checks and a Guarantor were catastrophic and extra money would have to be paid if he were to increase the tenancy past six months.

Moving day was a nightmare; Peter had accumulated loads of bottles of cleaning spray, all the same, and far more than he could physically use. Also, as his new flat was probably the same size but had a different layout, his furniture would not fit. We were moving things in and at the same time moving some items out again. Luckily, I was able to advertise the unwanted furniture on Gumtree and was able to claw back some money for Peter to make up for what he had to pay out for the rental of the flat. In many ways, this new flat was ideal, especially as he had an intercom system and everything was much newer, there were no teething problems, it was just around the corner from his previous flat, still local to town and Peter was very happy to be living there. The only disadvantage was that the space in the living area was considerably smaller, and this limited Peter as he still liked to pace around and twiddle his fiddle toys.

Whilst, he was living there, I began to do his cleaning and was able to keep up to date with his correspondence. This was an area that was always overlooked by his care workers.

When his move was completed, I began to worry about how long he would be there. Despite his autism, Peter coped with the move very well, but he couldn't carry on moving like this, and I was not getting any younger. I needed to consider other options and I approached adult services for an up-to-date assessment of his care needs.

Best Friend

Peter continued his friendship with his friend (from his Post 16 Provision) and he was now living in a care home. Peter was supported to visit this friend once a month, sometimes by car and at other times he was assisted with travel training (by train) as his friend lived about 30 miles away. They would spend a couple of hours together, chatting, watching films, and playing on the PlayStation. They also spoke several times a week on the phone and Peter was happy with this arrangement.

In September 2018, the friendship ended. This was a devastating blow for Peter as he had no idea why this had happened. His friend cut off all contact with him by phone and Facebook. Of course, we tried to support Peter as best as we could, but he was extremely angry with the situation. He wanted his friends, mum as his parent, his family were no longer important to him, and he changed his surname on Facebook to his friend's name. Even though Peter was 26, in his head he was experiencing things as if he were a teenager, where your friends are more important than anything else. He removed all family pictures from his flat and replaced them with pictures of his best friend.

The care agency that facilitated Peter's support was extremely concerned about his state of mind, so much that they were alerting adult services almost daily. We visited the doctors and were alerted to the learning disabilities doctor who increased his Pregabalin and prescribed Diazepam. This did not deaden the extreme responses that Peter was feeling. Peter told me that he was hitting himself over the head with a saucepan to try and become unconscious and begging the doctors to take him to the hospital. Despite all this, Peter would not return home so that we could keep an eye on him.

Peter was offered an appointment with the Clinical Psychologist he had once had dealings with, but he became angry and verbally violent towards her because she couldn't fix the situation. I suggested that it would be helpful if all of Peter's carers, staff at his supported volunteer placement, and myself be aware of the best way to assist Peter with the powerful emotions that he was feeling. People (including myself) kept giving him mixed advice based on what we would do in the same situation. Phrases such as 'move on' or 'calm down' were further agitating him and he was finding it difficult to make sense of his intense feelings. So, a letter was sent out advising everyone that had associations with Peter to allow him to have his own values and thoughts and not to unduly challenge him on these views. However, because this professional had said this directly to Peter, he took this advice quite literally and started voicing his opinions out in public, which led to people ostracising him and keeping their distance. He needed reassurance about what was against the law; this became quite important as he was constantly saying he was going to force his way into the care home where his friend lived. I found this advice liberating and I began to empathise with him by acknowledging that the situation must be upsetting for him. At times though, I felt that because I wanted to try and help him, I became frustrated that whatever I said to him made no difference and I spent many nights awake worrying about him.

We tried to allay his anxiety by persuading him to wait until his friend wanted to make contact again. This further exacerbated the problem as he was finding it increasingly difficult to wait for this to happen if indeed it ever would. We as adults would have mastered this technique, but this was far worse for Peter because of his autism and associated difficulties.

Peter made frequent visits independently to the town where his friend lived, in the hope of seeing him. In any normal situation, I would be proud of this independence, especially as it involved Peter changing trains, but it was the extreme desire that he was hoping to see his friend. He would also travel to wait outside his care home for the same reason.

Personal Independence Payment

As Peter was still on Disability Living Allowance, we were notified that it would be replaced with PIP (Personal Independence Payment). I had the laborious task of filling in the form, which for me must be completed over several weeks to ensure that I have considered how Peter's disability affects him. Any form that arrives, is completed by me as Peter cannot read successfully and is unable to fill in his own responses. This has remained a difficulty for Peter throughout his life, but I often allow him to give his responses verbally and sign most of his forms, but his handwriting continues to be very immature.

Once, the form had been filled in, we had to attend an assessment interview which I attended with him. It was just as well as it was not an easy place to find, even in a car, so for Peter to attempt this on his own may have proved a problem for him. Before this appointment, I had to stipulate who was attending with him and provide proof of my identity. I always request these appointments during school holidays (as I still work in the education sector), so that I can attend with him.

Following this assessment, Peter continued to be eligible for PIP at the Enhanced Rate for daily living needs and the Standard Rate for mobility. It is always a worry when attending these appointments that the accessor is ignorant of the individual struggles that a person has. Even though Peter is relatively good at articulating things of interest to him, he will often switch off during these assessments and start agreeing with whatever the person has said to him.

Capability for Work Assessment

Not long after Peter's assessment for PIP, we had to fill in another form for Employment Support Allowance and attend another interview. Peter was extremely anxious and agitated and the interview had to be stopped on several occasions. I was trying to let Peter respond to the questions asked but found myself interjecting as he was just repeating the same phrase back to the accessor and I didn't feel that she was understanding his difficulties. Similar things were asked of Peter to test his memory and understanding. For instance, spell the word 'world' backwards (which he couldn't do), fold a piece of paper in half (he just kept folding the paper over and over), memory recall of three items (this was successful), and spell his name backwards (he couldn't do). I find these tasks greatly inconsiderate as it only highlighted the fact that Peter was incapable of doing them which further increased his anxiety.

Once over, all we had to do was wait for the outcome.

Psychotic Episode

Peter's obsession with his friend continued and it was impacting his daily life. We were once called to the launderette where he did his washing as he was lying on the floor screaming and crying. He would not let us visit him in his flat and would only let me in to do his cleaning if he wasn't there. It started to affect his supported volunteer placement and the staff there were in touch with me weekly as they were becoming deeply concerned about his state of mind.

It came to a head one day when I received a call from the police. Peter had travelled a considerable way on the train and found his way to the college where his estranged friend was. He walked into the building, grabbed some lunch in the refectory, and then made his presence known to his friend. The staff at the college had no idea up to this point that an unknown person was on the premises. His friend did not want to see Peter and pushed him out of the way. Peter was there for many hours with the police, and they had not contacted me sooner as he had given out fake names and addresses. He told them that his friend was his brother, he gave someone else's name as his mum, his address was the town where his friend lived. The safeguarding officer at the college later told me that in her opinion he was having a psychotic episode and that he was terribly ill and should be taken to the doctors. She was happy for the doctor to contact her with regards to what went on. Fortunately, Peter was not charged with this incident, but I don't think it would have bothered him if they had. He started ranting about how useless the police were, how much he hated Theresa May and Donald Trump and he hated Sharon Osbourne because of her plastic surgery.

That evening, we made an emergency appointment with the doctor, and he prescribed an anti-psychotic drug called Aripiprazole. This was a low initial dose, which would be increased once the recommendation had been given by the learning disabilities doctor. It was hoped that Peter's obsession would be decreased by taking this drug, but he would need to be monitored by regular blood tests and ECGs. He was to take this drug along with his anti-anxiety drug, Pregabalin.

Nomad and Pill Dispenser

Peter had been collecting his prescriptions for some time with his medication dispensed into a Nomad (individual doses, daily for morning and evening). Peter had been managing this for a while, but often forgot to take his medication, which was worrying. Several years ago, adult services had previously decided that Peter should have a pill dispenser that would alert him and dispense the pills at the required time. Peter loves a bit of technology, but unfortunately, the pharmacy was unable to dispense them for him, so he had to put them into the machine himself. His carers seemed reluctant to complete this task or even to change the batteries when they were exhausted. However, Peter continued to move the pills from the Nomad to the pill dispenser himself, but it was becoming increasingly difficult as Peter was now on several pills at once. When cleaning, I would often find tablets on the floor that he had forgotten to take, and I alerted the care agency and adult services of this safe-guarding issue in the hope of gaining an up-to-date assessment of Peter's needs.

Social Worker

After nearly a year of chasing up an up-to-date assessment of Peter's needs, we eventually got an appointment with the social worker. We arranged it to take place after I had finished work one Friday afternoon.

There was so much to discuss regarding his care plan and the support given by the care agency. Upon arrival at the appointment, the Social Worker said that it would not take long. I remember thinking, you must be joking, there is much to discuss. Once she opened Peter's notes, she started remarking on his recent activity with regards to visiting his friend's college and about the police, but she went about it in completely the wrong way. Peter became very distressed and slammed his hand down on the table and starting ranting and raving about fat people, Theresa May, Donald Trump, and Sharon Osbourne. It was now evident that Peter would do this whenever he felt stressed, and I liken it to a form of Tourette's as the expletives would roll off his tongue. Another social worker joined us and between the two of them they managed to further increase his anxiety and they decided to stop the meeting.

During the weeks that followed, meetings were held without my knowledge, and changes to his care plan were made that decreased his hours. A follow-up appointment was promised but that did not happen until a year later.

Universal Credit

It was some weeks before I heard about the outcome of his Capability for Work Assessment, and I was shocked when I opened the envelope to say his Employment and Support Allowance had been stopped. These letters usually find their way through the letterbox on a weekend, where you are unable to do anything. I was told that he now needed to apply for Universal Credit and attend the job centre for work. This was unbelievable and I was deeply shocked by this result. My first job was to call ESA, the following Monday to appeal the decision and it took almost an hour to get through on the phone. I logged my appeal but also asked for the full report of the decision. When received, the report didn't match the tasks that Peter was asked to do and many discrepancies were found along with the comment that Peter was 'calm' at the meeting when in fact he was deeply distressed. I followed up my appeal with a letter outlining the errors and awaited their response.

Meanwhile, I had to apply for Universal Credit (UC) and attend an interview with Peter at the Job Centre. The lady there was unsympathetic to our needs, saying he must attend interviews and log into his UC account. I explained he would be unable to do these things without support and I would need time off work to attend with him, but she wouldn't listen; she was just following a script and was not mindful of the different needs of people. I must have started talking quite loudly because another lady took over the proceedings. She was able to see the issue I was having concerning Peter's disability, and she assisted me with the whole process.

Universal Credit needs to be applied for electronically by phone, tablet, or computer, where you can then log into your account, answer questions and make a note to the job centre by way of a journal entry. This was something I had to do for Peter and over the coming weeks, there was much to do from obtaining fit notes and providing evidence of his rent. Without, his ESA, he would need to start paying for his prescriptions, so in the interim, I purchased a pre-payment certificate to alleviate this stress for him. There would be no way that he could live independently if he were unable to find work and have no money coming in.

After a few weeks, I received notification that my appeal was successful and that Peter should not have come off ESA, but to continue UC with extra payments from ESA. What a result!

Despite this outcome, it took six weeks of chasing up payments before his full award was forthcoming. Following one of my calls, an official called and apologised for the delay. I thought, *Yes, I've waited six weeks, and it's not acceptable.* But he said, "I'm looking at a letter you sent several years ago and realise Peter should not have been moved to the support group on ESA, so you have a back payment coming to you." When received it was a substantial amount which was to come in very handy in the next few months as you will read about later.

Rowan Road

In May 2019, I had a hip replacement, and whilst recovering, I was able to log into the housing register (for Peter) to search for properties. This was something I did quite regularly, but as I was at home, I was able to go on the website, nice and early to search. Most of the time there were no properties, but one day, I found a flat that was close to the family home, and he was only number two in the queue. I was so excited, but nervous at the same time. I knew Peter had three months left on his current tenancy, so the move could be executed if he was successful. I went ahead and put in a bid and waited. I was notified a week later that he was unsuccessful. Even though I had this result, I was happy that I had done as much as I could and didn't reflect negatively on this outcome. A day later, however, came the news that the person that was number one in the queue had backed out, so that this meant Peter was now hopefully the intended occupant of this new flat. I was so happy, and Peter seemed thrilled at the result.

We went to see this flat, and it was in a very sorry state indeed, but it was decided that Andy, my husband could decorate, and with the back payment we could purchase carpets and kitchen goods and do a gradual move over the coming months. This did mean that Peter would be paying two lots of rent for a couple of months and again the back-dated pay that had been awarded a couple of months ago would come in handy; without this money, the move would not have been possible.

This timescale would also allow me time to organise the utilities change over and arrange for a broadband and tv package in addition to the various change of address notifications I needed to make.

Peter was unusually helpful during this whole process, especially as it lasted several months before he moved in. As before, there were far too many bottles of cleaning liquids that he had collected, but I was astounded at the amount of carrier bags that were in kitchen cupboards and his wardrobe. It was a nightmare! Also, as I hadn't been to clean his flat since my hip replacement, I found a mountain of unopened mail that needed sorting out along with requests for payment from NHS as he had ticked the wrong box for his prescriptions. I felt I was drowning in the number of things that I had to think about and do and I became quite stressed at the prospect of it all. For Peter, all this was a welcome distraction from his estranged friend, and he seemed to be turning a corner. For me, I was grateful that I was in the job I was because if I was working anywhere else other than a school, I simply would not have had the time to do everything that was required.

September came and Peter moved into his flat with the new carpets and appliances that he needed. It looked amazing, as Andy had done a fantastic job decorating. Over the coming months, new blinds were fitted, and Andy made a wardrobe in his bedroom. Now it was Peter's own flat, he could hang the pictures he wanted and there was loads of space for all his collectables.

Present Day Psychology

Peter continues to grieve for the loss of his friendship and despite the medication, he still has episodes of incredibly low mood. To try and help Peter come to terms with this predicament, he was referred to Psychology where he had several appointments with a Clinical Psychologist. Several options were presented to Peter to help him overcome the loss of his friend, but because they physically couldn't help him to get his friend back, he refused this help. He said talking about it made him more stressed. For me, I know how helpful talking therapies can be, but Peter was adamant that he didn't want to do this at the moment.

During one of these appointments, Peter told us of two people he had met on his group messenger chat, and they said they would try and get his friend back for him. These were people that were unknown to Peter, and they didn't live locally, so a chat followed about keeping himself safe online. It's difficult having this conversation with Peter; he doesn't understand his vulnerability and that there are people out there that are not who they say they are.

It was agreed that Peter's support help him to understand the threats of talking to unknown people online.

I would dearly have liked for Peter to take up the option of dealing with his grief because, without it, I fear he will be suffering for an exceptionally long time to come.

Coronavirus

At this time (March 2020), we have a pandemic called the Coronavirus, which has caused multiple deaths around the world. This means that we must socially isolate ourselves from people that do not live in our normal household. A message came on Friday, that all schools are to close, except for keyworkers and then the following Monday, we were told that we should not leave the house except for one period of physical exercise, such as walking or riding a bike, and essential travel to work.

I had to present this current situation to Peter, which he did not take well at first. He had already been told that he could not visit his girlfriend in the care home and his supported volunteer opportunities had been suspended. However, once he realised that everyone else was the same, he seemed much calmer.

As Peter had been highlighted as a vulnerable adult by adult services, I was informed that he would receive welfare calls periodically to help alleviate any anxieties he may be feeling and Zoom calls from his supported volunteer placement. Even though we were told not to mix with anyone not in our household, I felt I had to relax that restriction for Peter. So, during this time I still cleaned his flat, whilst he was out for a walk. I helped with shaving and other personal care that normally gets sorted by the hairdressers or a chiropodist. As the launderette was closed, I assisted with his washing by bringing it home and delivering it the following week. I made sure that his fridge was full of healthy food in the unfortunate event that his meal support was cancelled due to the spread of the virus.

For Peter, this has been a period of high anxiety due to not being able to see his girlfriend or friends, but he does make use of Messenger to have a group chat which has helped to keep his sanity.

Discretionary Trust

There comes a time when you begin to reflect on what will happen when you die. There is so much to think about regarding finances and putting things in place that will make life easier for my daughter Stephanie. It's hard to think about a time when you will no longer be around to assist, and it saddens and worries me.

If this is something that resonates with you, then my advice is to get it sorted sooner rather than later. I have been incredibly lucky to have had a solicitor that has helped me through this rather tough decision. It would be very difficult to leave Peter any money as he would not be able to manage it for himself, so it was agreed that a Discretionary Trust would be set up as part of my will for Peter to have the money as my executors see fit. This would protect his benefits and the money would be safe.

I have also successfully, completed a Lasting Power of Attorney so that when I pass my daughter will be able to manage his money in the same way as I have been responsible for. A solicitor can do this for you, but I have found that it's quite simple to do on the Direct.gov website and dispense with the huge costs that solicitors charge.

Learning Disability
Forensic Team

Another form of support was offered to Peter from The Forensic Community Learning Disabilities Team designed to assist people with learning disabilities from offending, which is a real risk for Peter. Whilst, visiting at home, rather than in the clinic (due to the Coronavirus), they noted the difficulty that Peter was experiencing regarding his estranged friend. Despite the time that has elapsed since the friendship has ended; it was and still is extremely hard to change his thinking. As I was unable to get time off work for this appointment, it was decided that support from his care agency attend and feedback to me accordingly. This is made possible due to a freedom of information declaration that Peter has signed. This enables me to have conversations with regards to Peter with his supported volunteer placement, social workers, general practitioners, and his care agency.

It was decided at this appointment that a custody passport should be completed. This is a relatively new document that would explain Peter's needs in the unfortunate event of him being arrested. Because of Peter's literal interpretation of spoken language, he could become quite vocal and aggressive, and this document would help explain his needs and allow for the necessity of having an appropriate adult to help with the overwhelming situation should it ever arise. It is worth saying that Peter means no harm to anyone, but because of his autism, he finds it difficult to distinguish between the anger he thinks he feels, when in fact, I believe it's more distress and anxiety that is fuelling his emotions.

The problem that arises during these appointments without me being present is the information that Peter gives with regard to his medication. He will often say he is on a drug when he isn't even though the prescriber should know this information. For instance, his anti-anxiety medication was withdrawn to be replaced with a higher dose of his anti-psychotic drug, but Peter incorrectly reported this to his Consultant Psychiatrist. There are some concerns about his lack of ability to make decisions where his medication is concerned, he will often just agree with whatever is said to him for an easy life. He does know, however, that his medication helps him, and he understands why he is being prescribed it. I feel reassured that when changes are made, he knows that it's in his best interests.

Final Word

My account has now come to an end and writing it has been hugely rewarding and sometimes upsetting. As a mother, I hope I have done my best for Peter, but know that my determination has not been welcomed by him at times. It's not that I am a control freak, it's just that I prefer to be proactive instead of being reactive. If something needs doing, I don't put it off and I cannot enjoy what I am doing unless I know that Peter is happy. Of course, not everyone is the same and many of you who have autistic children or adults may well steer a better course than the one I have embarked on. My advice, however, is not to always trust what is being said and if you feel things are not right, then challenge it. Sometimes it is easier to go for an easy life but in my experience, it has mostly helped me to get the required outcome.

In the past, before Peter, I think I was a selfish individual, but he has quite simply made me a better person. The lows have been low and it almost destroyed me, on the other hand, I have realised that I must be quite resilient which I've only felt since writing this account.

For Stephanie, I worry. She has seen first-hand the struggles that we have endured as a family, and I know she is very apprehensive as to what will happen when I am not around. She has a young family herself and knows that she would not have the 'headspace' to deal with the issues that Peter still faces. Hopefully, I will be around for a while yet and by then her family will be a little older, and that is why I have tried to put as much in place as I can.

Even though he continues to have difficulties with his broken friendship, I am so proud of the adult he has become. Managing to live independently is a real achievement and one that I didn't think he would ever be able to do. He has some lovely friends, which he is extremely loyal to, a lovely girlfriend that makes him so happy and full of life. That's all you ever want for your children, and I feel privileged that this story has been mine to tell.

Useful Information

Family Fund

www.familyfund.org.uk

National Autistic Society

www.autism.org.uk

Personal Independence Payment (PIP)

www.gov.uk

Universal Credit

www.gov.uk

Parking Badge

www.gov.uk

Mind

www.mind.org.uk

Special Olympics

www.specialolympics.org

Kids

www.kids.org.uk

Power of Attorney

www.gov.uk

Cinema Exhibitors Card

https://www.ceacard.co.uk

https://www.telecarechoice.co.uk
https://pecs-unitedkingdom.com
https://enablingtechnology.com
https://www.carecalls.co.uk
https://www.breakawaysupportedholidays.co.uk

The Right to Work CIC

www.therighttowork.co.uk

Mike Davies,
Independent Educational Neuropsychologist,
HCPC Registered
michaelndavies@talk21.com